GW00362051

POCKET IMAGES

The Cornish Coast

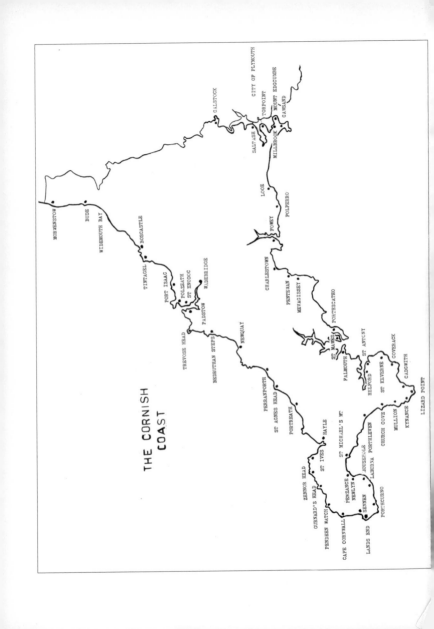

THE CORNISH COAST

POCKET IMAGES

The Cornish Coast

Tom Bowden

NONSUCH

To my wife Pam for her support and wise counsel

First published 1994
This new pocket edition 2007
Images unchanged from first edition

Nonsuch Publishing
Cirencester Road, Chalford
Stroud, Gloucestershire, GL6 8PE
www.nonsuch-publishing.com

Nonsuch Publishing is an imprint of NPI Media Group

British Library Cataloguing in Publication Data.
A catalogue record for this book is available from the British Library.

ISBN 978-1-84588-412-3

Typesetting and origination by NPI Media Group
Printed in Great Britain

Contents

Penhale Point near Newquay, 1941.

Introduction

I have a tendency to flick through picture books without reading the introduction. After all, why bother with the starter when the main course has been served? So in asking you to read these few words I am being a little contradictory. I just want to explain what I have tried to achieve with this book.

Cornwall, my home county, is really beyond description, with its history and people, its grand cliffs, lovely harbours and sandy bays. Many writers try to describe it with wonderful photography and superb words, but with varying degrees of success. You might even think that only a fool would try to show the Cornish coast in old photographs.

In this book we travel from Calstock on the quiet River Tamar to Plymouth Sound and around the south and north coasts to end at Morwenstow where the Revd Robert Hawker, a Plymouth man, wrote the Cornish anthem 'Trelawny'. I don't pretend to sail the coast, or walk, or drive around; I just get there.

Basically, I have collected over 200 old postcards of locations around the Cornish coast. They cover a period of about eighty years, from the 1890s to the 1970s. The subjects include cliffs, harbours, beaches, coves, ships, churches, rivers, pubs and houses, with people at work and play, and give a visual impression of an earlier age.

My view is that a picture without words can be beautiful and thought-provoking, but tends to leave questions in the mind. Where is it? Who is he? Why are they doing that? So a good caption answers some of those questions in a few words and maybe adds some information to get the maximum from the picture. I have attempted to achieve that objective.

I should explain why these particular photographs have been chosen to show the coast of Cornwall. First of all, they were available from my collection. Also, some Cornish people seem to believe that Cornwall starts at Bodmin! Therefore,

hese are the sands we bathe from. They are s inn we can play dennis on them. I hope you are enjoying yourself as much as I am. Best love P.S. a

Bishop Rock, Newquay, 1900.

in starting at Calstock my aim is to highlight the border and people who live there. Conversely, who in east Cornwall knows the small coves in Penwith? So I hope there will be something of interest to everyone.

Frankly, the distribution of locations is strongly influenced by my background. You will see some emphasis on Torpoint, Looe and Porthleven, where I have family connections. I think that is acceptable because the people we meet there are typical of Cornish people everywhere.

You will realize that, with the limitations imposed by this Old Photograph series, I am probably unable to include your favourite little cove or harbour, where you spent such happy days. So I hope you will excuse me.

In writing the captions I sometimes give way to my sense of the ridiculous, my feelings of joy or sorrow, and sometimes my anger over lost young lives. I hope there is some scholarship too, and no 'hobby horses' or wild flights of fancy.

Lastly, I have enjoyed compiling this book about all those places in the Cornwall that I love. I hope you like it too.

Tom Bowden

One

Calstock to Cremyll

The lovely River Tamar at full tide in 1906, winding its way to Calstock where we start our journey around the Cornish coast.

Calstock, 1907. The Saltash, Three Towns & District Steamboat Company paddle steamer *Alexandria* passing Calstock parish quay on its way downstream. This was a graceful 127-ft long 125-ton steel vessel built in 1888. The company ran these river trips to the traditional destinations of Calstock, Morwellham and Wier Head and stopped for cream teas on the way. Calstock was coming to the end of its prosperity with the local mines: Calstock Consoles, Okel Tor, Danescombe and Cotehele Consoles were all closing. Today it is a pleasant place with its steep slopes and narrow streets. The sixteenth-century Boot Inn is still open and the Riverside Restaurant still welcomes boat trips from the Barbican in Plymouth in the summer months.

Oppposite above: Calstock, 1916. You can see the elegant Calstock viaduct which carries the Gunnislake–Plymouth railway line. It was constructed in 1906–7, is 117 ft high with twelve spans, and 'flies' over the old town. It is hard to believe that it's constructed of concrete blocks which were cast on the Devon bank of the river! The tower on the left is a wagon hoist which was installed at the same time to provide a means of transporting goods between the quay and the railway line.

Below: Calstock from the Ashburton Hotel, c. 1915 (now the Danescombe Hotel). A cargo ship is alongside Calstock Quay loading with minerals or stone from the local quarries. The quay stretched for three-quarters of a mile at that time and there were piles of copper stacked on the quay awaiting shipment. In 1860 an incline railway was built from the high ground down to the quay for better transport of goods in either direction.

The granite south tower and gatehouse of Cotehele House, seen in 1960, by the River Tamar near Calstock. William Edgcumbe married Hileria de Cotehele, the heiress to the Cotehele estate, in 1353. His famous grandson, Richard Edgcumbe, inherited Cotehele House in about 1460. He built this south gateway and tower and made other changes. He supported the Lancastrians in the Wars of the Roses and feuded with Sir Henry Bodrugan, a 'Yorkist' freebooter from Chapel Cross near Mevagissey. Sir Richard's son, Piers, married Joan Durnford, the heiress to the Stonehouse lands overlooking Plymouth Sound, including what became Mount Edgcumbe on the Cornish side. In 1553 the family moved to a grand new home, 12 miles down the river, at Mount Edgcumbe. Now Cotehele House, with its charming gardens, woods, chapel and quay on the Tamar, is in the care of the National Trust and open to visitors. It is one of the best-preserved medieval houses in Britain.

Opposite above: The east front of Cotehele House. This has a splendid view over the terrace garden, medieval dovecot and valley garden to the river.

Opposite below: The River Tamar near Calstock, c. 1906. The river loops like a snake from Gunnislake Weir, past Morwellham, Calstock, Cotehele, Halton Quay, Cargreen and Landulph to Saltash. There are barges and schooners passing and the scenery is beautiful, with the Tamar ebbing and flowing and wading birds feeding on the exposed mudflats. At the turn of the century there were many prosperous copper, tin and arsenic mines in this area with interesting railways, canals, tunnels, slopes and quays for the transport of their produce down the river to Plymouth and beyond.

Pentillie Castle and River Tamar, c. 1905. The river takes one last mighty wiggle before heading south. Pentillie Castle is high up on the bend, to the left.

The Royal Albert Bridge at Saltash, 1904. It was completed by I.K. Brunel in 1859 and is thought to be his best railway achievement. The River Tamar is some 1,100 ft wide and 70 ft deep at this point, and the Navy required that the single rail track be 100 ft above the water to allow passage for shipping. Brunel decided on this design to meet these requirements, and to confine the deep underwater work to the one central column. The bridge was opened by Prince Albert in May 1859. Brunel died in September of that year at the age of fifty-three after battling with his leviathan, the *Great Eastern*.

The Ferry Bridge, Saltash.

Above: Saltash Steam Ferry, c. 1919. Note the horse-drawn transport and the gas lighting, with a man up a ladder doing maintenance work. A ferry service was started here in 1356 and later this type of chain ferry was used. When the new road bridge was completed in 1961 the ferry was taken out of service, to the annoyance of many local people.

Right: Tamar Street, Saltash, c. 1930. Butcher Cory is standing in his doorway with his child while the great bridge throws its shadow overhead. The white cottage on the left was knocked down in the 1930s and a detached house was built on the site but set back from the road.

HMS *Defiance*, c. 1903. Moored in the River Lynher off Wearde Quay, near Saltash, *Defiance* was the Royal Navy's Torpedo School. The ships forming the school sometimes changed, but I think here they comprise *Defiance* on the right, with *Perseus* in the middle (with a tender alongside), and *Flamingo* on the left. HMS *Defiance* was built at Pembroke in 1861, a wooden ship of 5,270 tons, but with the advent of ironclad ships she was already obsolete. She was laid up at Devonport until 1884 when she was commissioned at Wearde Quay as the Torpedo School ship. In 1931 the original *Defiance*, then seventy years old, was withdrawn, then sold and broken up in Millbay Docks, Plymouth. The school was finally closed down in 1959.

North front of Antony House near Torpoint, c. 1905. It is the home of the famous Carew family and was built by Sir William Carew between 1718 and 1729. It looks out over a romantic landscape to the rivers Lynher and Tamar at Antony Passage, with Trematon Castle across the river.

South front of Antony House, c. 1905. Observe, from these two views of the house, how the ugly east wing ruins its symmetry. Lt.-Gen. Sir Reginald Pole-Carew had the wing built, and he was horrified when he saw it on returning from service overseas. After the Second World War his son, Sir John Carew Pole, had the offending appendage removed. The house is now in the care of the National Trust.

Portrait of Sir Alexander Carew in Antony House. He was on Cromwell's side during the Civil War (1642–6) and was made Governor of St Nicholas Island (now Drake's Island) in Plymouth Sound during the siege of the city by the king's men. The Cornish Royalist army was victorious throughout the West Country in 1643. Alexander must have been concerned for the safety of his family. He brooded alone and finally decided to change sides. A servant revealed Alexander's intentions; he was arrested in August 1643 and beheaded at Tower Hill, London, on 23 December 1644. The portrait has a row of stitches around the canvas. It is thought that the family cut the picture from its frame when Alexander joined Cromwell, and replaced it when he turned to the king.

Torpoint Ferry Beach, 1900. A look at the foreshore—from one of the ferries, I believe. The two chains on the right-hand side of the beach disappear underground and into the structure behind; the chains are attached to weights which hang inside and take up any slack in the chain. On the extreme right there is a pontoon for passengers of small ferries and pleasure boats.

Torpoint Ferry, 1894. There has been a ferry at Torpoint since about 1730 but it was not until 1834 that James Meadows Rendel built the first ferry with a steam engine to pull it across the river on chains and beat the tides. The ferry is on the Devonport side and Torpoint is in the distance with Gravesend House and The Lawn on the right. Today there are three diesel-driven ferries, among the biggest river ferries in the world, but there are still long queues at times!

Torpoint Ferry and the Hamoaze, c. 1900. More horses and carts and ladies in long dresses. Devonport and the dockyard are in the distance with a nineteenth-century sailing ship. A naval cutter is going by with a group of gasping matelots pulling at the oars. A good exercise in teamwork, but you end up with blistered hands and a raw bottom!

Torpoint Ferry, 1916. The five-masted ship behind the ferry is interesting. There were three like that built in the 1860s: the *Minotaur*, *Agincourt* and *Northumberland*. They were 400 ft long, with a single propeller, and displaced 10,690 tons. For ten years these were the biggest ships afloat, with the heaviest armament, behind the thickest armour and with the highest sea speed. The *Northumberland* was placed in reserve in Devonport in 1891 so that must be the one we see here. Go on, tell me it's two ships, side by side!

The Hamoaze from Torpoint.

The Hamoaze from Torpoint, 1904. There is a mixture of attractive but outdated wooden ships and ironclad warships in harbour, and the horses wait patiently for the ferry. Reginald Carew had planned the building of Torpoint on his land, across the Tamar from the growing dockyard, in the 1770s. It was then built in a gridiron pattern and gradually grew. It is thought the name Torpoint came about because boats were tarred on the shore, and Torpoint is a corruption of 'tar point'.

Above and below: Two views of Fore Street, Torpoint. The bottom photograph was taken in 1911 and looks up the street from outside the Wheeler's Arms. Just a few horses and carts, with a lady talking to a shopkeeper. The top picture was taken further up the street in 1930. That looks like the embryo Co-op on the left, the noble Lloyds Bank building is further up on the corner, the Wesleyan Church is on the right, while another pub is down at the other end.

Ellis Memorial in Torpoint, c. 1905. The monument was erected in 1900 in memory of James Benjamin Ellis who lost his life in July 1897 saving two boys from drowning when they got into difficulties while bathing near Torpoint Ballast Pond. Later a neat little park was completed around the memorial. It is said that it got the name of Sparrow Park because a local reporter attended the opening ceremony and commented in his paper that the park was so small it was only fit for sparrows! That's how it is known today.

Grandad sharpening a saw. This was taken in about 1938 when he was fifty-nine. We all lived in Navy Terrace down by the river. It's gone all posh now and become Marine Drive. Grandad was very good at sharpening saws. He was also good at growing tomatoes, except when I picked them all while still dark green!

Gran and the boys having their picture taken in 1938. I'm about nine and brother Jim is four. Grandad said 'watch the birdie', but Jim saw a 'creepy-crawly' in the bushes, and this is the result. Grandad either ran out of film or stamped off muttering! So all we have is this imperfect picture. Now I'm a grandfather myself, and I look at the picture and see a proud grandmother with naughty kids, and I think it's fine.

Dad and me in a boat in 1934. Dad was a skilled craftsman and built a number of boats. He sailed his 14-ft international class dinghy, the Restless, at regattas, and later when I was older we went out 'wiffing' for mackerel in the harbour.

Torpoint Benefactor of Mankind Lodge, c. 1918. This was a branch of the Independent Order of Good Templars, a friendly society of various ages dedicated to mutual self-help. Here they are in their regalia in the garden of Salamanca House, Torpoint, the home of Mr and Mrs J. Hyslop. Jim Hyslop is seated immediately behind the table. His wife Beatrice is also in that row and fourth from the left, and Fred Roberts is fifth from the left. My mum, then Emma Woodrow Devereux, is seated cross-legged by the table in front of Mr Roberts. Salamanca House is on one side of Eliot Square, alongside St James' Parish Church, with Salamanca Street running behind the house and down to the river. Over the years, hundreds of happy couples have emerged from the church on their wedding day to have their photograph taken in this pretty garden, thanks to the kindness of the owners. Eliot Square is named after Sir John Eliot of Port Eliot House, St Germans, who opposed Charles I before the Civil War (1642–6), was imprisoned in the Tower of London and died there in 1629. I like the fellow standing in the back row on the left. He's waited long enough for this photographer and his attention is beginning to wander.

St James' Church, Torpoint, c. 1910. The parish church in Eliot Square with Salamanca House on the left. The children watch the photographer and the horses have been and gone.

Copyright
Lilywhite(1932)Ltd.
Sowerby Bridge.

North Road, Torpoint.

Antony Road in Torpoint, c. 1932 (not North Road as captioned). It's the main road out of Torpoint leading to Antony. On the right is Jimmy Devonshire's garage with those artistic petrol pumps. The road name changes to Fore Street at the bottom of the hill.

The Lawn, Torpoint, 1920. The Lawn then had a tea hut and families would come from miles around for an enjoyable time. The kids would swim, or play in the muddy sand, or climb trees in the woods, and eat sweets and ice-cream. Unfortunately, after the war it was decided that the pool was a danger to health and the authorities filled it in and turfed it.

Pottery Road, Torpoint, 1910. Alexandra Terrace is in the foreground, with the workhouse behind the large tree, and Chapeldown Road in the distance. There is a nice sunny outlook over the water to Maker Heights. Apart from improvements to the road, the only major change today is that the workhouse has been knocked down and replaced by two blocks of flats.

Millbrook Lake, 1904. See the old tide mill and millpond, with All Saints' Church nearby. There are brick-works and quarries at Foss and Southdown, and on Maker Heights you can see the 65-ft tower of Maker Church. Today the brick-works have closed, the millpond is filled in and the land reclaimed as a recreation area. The upper reaches of the lake have been dammed as part of the flood prevention scheme.

SOUTH DOWN AND HAMOAZE, DEVONPORT.

The Hamoaze and Southdown, 1918. In the nineteenth century most of Millbrook's industries had been in the Southdown area. There was a gunpowder mill, soap factory, copper smelter, brewery, fish fertilizer works and glue factory at various times, and it must have been an odorous place. By 1918 most of these industries had closed or were in decline.

Above and below: Cremyll Point and HMS *Impregnable*, 1906. Two views of Cremyll Point, the narrowest point in the harbour, where there is a ferry service to the Plymouth side. In ancient times it formed part of a route into Cornwall. The Edgcumbe Arms is on the quay and the naval training ship *Impregnable* is moored offshore. The pub got very busy with passing trade, and with many naval customers carousing at weekends. Today the ferry service is still in operation and the Edgcumbe Arms is still serving customers while they enjoy the lovely harbour views, but the Tower House was demolished by a bomb in 1941. The naval training ships have long disappeared to a breaker's yard, and I have heard it said that the hulks provided Cremyll with shelter from the easterly winds; when they were removed in the 1920s the climate changed!

Two

Mount Edgcumbe to Talland

The Hamoaze viewed from Empacombe, near Mount Edgcumbe, 1904. In the distance is the Royal Albert Bridge at Saltash. Torpoint is on the left, and the *Impregnable* and the old naval dockyard on the right. Those covered slipways in the dockyard date from the early nineteenth century. The area was then named Plymouth Dock, and it wasn't until 1824 that the name was changed to Devonport.

Valentine's Series

Mount Edgcumbe House, c. 1910. Piers, the son of the legendary Sir Richard Edgcumbe, married Joan Durnford, heiress to the Stonehouse lands. He thus inherited land on both sides of the Tamar, including Mount Edgcumbe Park. His son, Sir Richard Edgcumbe, built Mount Edgcumbe House and in 1553 the family moved there from Cotehele. The house was designed as a compact building without a courtyard and it became one of the great Elizabethan houses. On 21 April 1941, during the Plymouth blitz, incendiary bombs fell on the house and it was completely gutted. In 1958 Kenelm Edgcumbe, the 6th Earl, completed rebuilding. Today the house and country park, covering 864 acres, are owned jointly by Plymouth City Council and Cornwall County Council and are open to the general public. Thousands of people enjoy this beautiful place each year.

A front view of Mount Edgcumbe House and lawn, 1900.

The Folly in Mount Edgcumbe Park, with Drake's Island and Plymouth Hoe in the distance, 1909. The Folly was built by Richard, 1st Baron Mount Edgcumbe, in 1747 as one of the attractions in the park. Before this he had been MP for Plympton in Devon for forty years, a favourite of George II, and had held important positions in the Treasury. Richard was fond of his dog, and when the animal died he put its skeleton into the garden house so he could gaze at his old pal!

Lady Emma's cottage, 1907. Lady Emma was the wife of George, the 1st Earl of Mount Edgcumbe. The original cottage was built in about 1790; it was later destroyed by fire, and this cottage was built in 1876. In 1789 George III and Queen Charlotte had come, with a grand fleet, to visit Sir George and Emma Edgcumbe at Mount Edgcumbe, and George was created the 1st Earl of Mount Edgcumbe for his services to the king.

Barn Pool and Temple of Milton, c. 1911. The temple is probably another of the 1st Baron's additions to the park. It is an elegant Ionic rotunda standing at Barn Pool on Plymouth Sound. Barn Pool is a pretty cove on the estate near Cremyll, and the ferry used to run from here years ago.

Picklecombe Fort, c. 1910. This is one of Palmerston's follies, built in 1871. It was fitted with 10-in guns and, with Bovisand and Breakwater forts, was capable of protecting the Sound with a blanket of gunfire, which was never required. It was retained by the military until 1956. Later the fort was converted into flats which now provide homes with lovely views over the Sound.

Cawsand in the relatively quiet 1920s. There are two adjoining villages in Cawsand Bay, Cawsand and Kingsand, and they were very busy before the Plymouth breakwater was completed by Sir John Rennie in 1841. This was because it was easier for ships to be victualled there rather than send boats all the way to Plymouth. So there are many fine eighteenth-century houses built on the steep slopes and along the tortuous roadways. It must have been an exciting and dangerous place in the heyday of smuggling and fishing, the ale houses busy with sailors from ships at anchor in the bay. The locals had to dodge press-gangs and excisemen too!

Whitsand Main Beach and Rame Head, c. 1910. We are looking east towards Plymouth; I think we are on Sharrow Point with Freathy Beach immediately ahead, followed by Main Beach, Treganhawke Beach, Polhawn Cove, and with the unmistakable outline of Rame Head on the skyline.

Main Beach in Whitsand Bay, c. 1910. This is sometimes referred to as Withnoe Beach. This is a view from the top of the path leading down on to the sands. It was the favourite beach because it had a tea-hut and donkey rides—and the easiest path to climb at the end of the day.

Fun on Whitsand, c. 1910. We have just clambered down on to Main Beach and found a place to sit. That's Willcock's tea-house in the background. The adults didn't take their clothes off in 1910! Long skirts, suits and waistcoats were the fashion then. What a difference now!

The Grotto at Sharrow Point, 1910. It is just a little cave in the rocks with nice views over Whitsand Bay. The ladies seem to like the sun (or have posed for the camera), while the gentleman is inside trying to read the limericks on the walls.

Portwrinkle and the Whitsand Bay Hotel, c. 1912. Further west around Whitsand Bay we come to Portwrinkle which comprises two coves, a few cottages, and this hotel. The beaches are of shingle and sand, and children love looking for crabs in the rock pools. The Gothic-style Whitsand Bay Hotel has an interesting history. It was once the home of the Graves family, and was sited in Torpoint. They were descendants of Admiral Graves who led a division at the great sea battle off Ushant in 1794. In 1909 it was sold and dismantled stone by stone and re-erected here in Portwrinkle in 1910. Today it is the Whitsand Bay Hotel and Golf Club.

Downderry, c. 1945. A view looking west towards Looe with gardens of bungalows stretching down to the sea. In the middle distance is the Inn on the Beach, and a scattering of shops. A nice quiet place to retire to, after working for years in the city.

Seaton, 1935. More correctly, Seaton on the left and the west end of Downderry on the right. Seaton hasn't changed very much. It is at the mouth of Hessenford valley and has this wide expanse of beach with a river running down through it in a haphazard way. There is a group of shops and a car park, and plenty of sand to play on. Since 1935 there have been a number of holiday parks here but they have all disappeared.

Looe from above Marine Drive, 1910. East Looe is on the right and West Looe on the left, joined by the bridge built in 1856. This was the end of the copper boom period and you can see Buller (or Copper) Quay on the right, which had previously been full of copper ore awaiting shipment. St Nicholas' Church in West Looe is seen at the bottom left with The Downs up on the top left-hand side.

Looe from the Downs, 1910. A lovely view downriver, with St Nicholas' Church in the foreground and Hannafore Road wriggling out along the harbour side to become Marine Drive on reaching Hannafore. On East Looe is the famous Banjo Pier and the ancient tower of St Mary's Church. It was built in 1257 and whitewashed to become a 'daymark' for mariners, so it remained all this time while the church itself has been rebuilt three times! In 1737 they fitted a clock on the tower which had only one hand. It sounds like a familiar cost-cutting story: save £5, and no one can tell the time! There are four phases in the history of Looe. In biblical times the locals traded tin with the Phoenicians, and in medieval times the Bodrigan family held sway. Then the copper boom came with the discovery of copper at Caradon Hill nearby in about 1840. By the early twentieth century the copper had gone, and now there is a fishing fleet and the place is crammed with tourists in the high season.

Opposite below: The Millpond and West River at Looe, c. 1910. Thomas Arundell, younger son of an Arundell of Trerice, bought a 600-year lease of 13 acres of estuary in 1614 and enclosed it with a curving 700-yd wall. He built this mill house, with water-wheel and lock gates, and it worked for many years as a grist mill. The lease has not yet run out! Today a large part of the lake has been filled in to form a car park.

Old Looe fishermen, c. 1900. Left to right: Tommy Toms, Sam Organ, Climo, Capt. Salt, Fred Soady, Harry Toms, Bob Prynn, Ben Menhenick, Jim Toms.

A group of Looe fishermen about the turn of the century. Back row, left to right: Edgar Toms, John Edward Pengelly, George Frederick Woodrow Pengelly. Front: Walter Toms, Alf Soady, Leo Prynn.

Sailing luggers leaving harbour, 1910. They were going to sea for a night's fishing, and the families were on the pier to wave them goodbye. No motors in those days, just the sails or the oars. Most of the luggers were drifting for pilchards. On their return to harbour the catch was salted down in brine for several weeks. Then the pilchards were pressed into barrels and exported to Italy.

Fisherman Richard Pengelly of East Looe, c. 1908. Richard was born in 1833 and married Emma Woodrow of Morval in 1854. They included the name 'Woodrow' in the Christian names of their children (when they remembered) and became one of the Pengelly family groups in Looe. There are a lot of Pengellys in Looe! Here we see Richard sitting on an anchor on Buller Quay with some of his sons and grandsons.

Above, left and right: Two views of a little street in Looe c. 1910. How did they dry their washing in these cramped streets? Well, they got this 30-ft Cornish giant 'Comshanger' to come and hang it on the roof! Seriously, it must have been very hard work boiling the clothes and hanging them out. The photograph on the left shows a view looking down Lower Market Street on wash-day. The house on the corner has a plaque stating it was built in 1456 and is the oldest house in Looe. I think the right-hand photograph shows Lower Market Street from the other end. Note the typical fisherman's cottage part way along. The family live upstairs in dry conditions while nets, etc., are stored downstairs where dampness or flooding may occur.

Opposite above: East Looe and the tower of St Nicholas' Church, 1906. St Nicholas' was built about the end of the thirteenth century and is dedicated to St Nicholas, Bishop of Myra. At times in the past it has been used as a guild-hall for West Looe, and people have been tried and imprisoned in the building. Across the river can be seen the guild-hall built in 1878 and the fish market on the quay. The railway station and old canal, both leading to Liskeard, are up past the bridge and on the east side of the river.

Below: The Jolly Sailor, c. 1918. There are still three fifteenth-century pubs in Looe. This one in West Looe, and the Fisherman's Arms and the Salutation Inn in East Looe. The Salutation has a sloping floor to let high spring tide waters drain out quickly. It can be very confusing, mixing strong drink with water and sloping floors!

The Old Bridge at Looe. An engraving of this splendid fifteen-arch bridge which was built in 1411, just downstream of the present bridge. Note the curious diversity of its arches. The Old Bridge had a 6-ft roadway and was inadequate for the busy copper trade. In 1856 a new bridge with a 12-ft carriageway was built and the old one demolished. Then the road bridge was widened to 24 ft in 1960 to meet the demands of modern traffic.

Opposite above: The Banjo Pier in Looe, 1929. The original pier, known as the groyne, was built about 1850. Unfortunately, it did not prevent sand from the beach entering the harbour. Engineer Joseph Thomas proposed that a round end be added to the pier, and said he would forego a fee if it didn't work. The round was added in 1898 and it was completely successful. Inevitably, the groyne soon became known as the banjo pier. See how the washing has been laid on the hillside to dry. This was before a promenade had been built along the front. My grandmother used to live in a house on the front and when there was a bad storm the sea water used to come in the front door and go out the back!

Below: The pier at Looe, c. 1909. Edwardian Looe with ships gathered for a regatta day perhaps?

45

The bathing beach at Looe, c. 1920. The beach at East Looe faces south and has all the necessary amenities close at hand. Mum and dad can even sit on the promenade and keep an eye on things.

Looe Island and Hannafore, 1910. Looking west from here you can see Joseph Thomas' Banjo Pier and the road he drove out through West Looe to Hannafore in 1895. About half a mile off shore is privately owned Looe Island.

Talland Bay, c. 1910. A very pretty bay with rocks and a small sandy beach, all approached via narrow country lanes which now get very congested in the summer-time. The little winding road goes to Porthallow up over the hill, and Talland Church can be seen on the hillside.

Talland Church, c. 1910. This beautiful and unique church dates back to the thirteenth century, and is dedicated to St Tallanus, probably a local lady saint. The 55-ft tower stands detached from the body of the church, and looks out over the shore. My Irish great-grandfather is buried in the churchyard and the inscription reads: 'In Sacred Memory Martin Devereux Age 33 Died 13th March 1873. For he knoweth our frame he remembereth that we are dust. Psalm MCIII 14th verse'. He was married in Talland Church in 1866, and buried there in 1873.

Inside Talland Church, c. 1910. The south aisle has a magnificent fifteenth-century wagon roof, and many well-carved bench ends of the same period. In the south-east corner is John Bevill's intricately carved slate tomb chest dated 1578. He was an ancestor of Elizabeth Bevill, the mother of Bevill Grenville.

Three

Polperro to
St Anthony in Meneage

Pretty Polperro Harbour, 1937. This is one of the most quaint fishing villages in Cornwall. It lies in a steep-sided valley and has narrow streets and a picturesque harbour with two piers. The massive Peak Rock gives protection on the west side.

Rowing boats at Polperro, 1930. An atmospheric scene with ladies hanging out their washing and fishermen pottering around in rowing boats, perhaps preparing for another night at sea.

Busy Polperro Harbour, c. 1910. Fishing boats are in harbour and nets are strewn around. You can see the steep valley in the background. Smuggling and fishing appear to have been Polperro's main activities in the nineteenth century, and as these things have declined it has become a haunt of artists and tourists. A large car park has been provided at the top of the town and cars are virtually banned from the village.

Fowey Harbour.

Lovely Fowey Harbour, c. 1915. Fowey town is on the west side and Polruan on the east. The harbour is very busy with an assortment of elegant steam- and wind-driven vessels. Out of view, the river wends up to Lostwithiel, passing Pont Pill, Bodinnick, Golant and Lerryn on its way. The parish church of St Finbarrus is dedicated to Fin Barr of Cork. In 1456 the French burnt the town, including the Norman church, and the new church and tower were built in 1465. St Catherine's Castle at the mouth of the west side of the harbour was built by Thomas Treffry of Place in 1538–42 as ordered by Henry VIII. Behind the castle is the Rashleigh Mausoleum built by William Rashleigh of Point Neptune. Scholar and novelist Sir Arthur Quiller-Couch (1863–1944) lived in The Haven on the shore side of the Esplanade. At the top of the hill in Polruan you can see St Saviour's Point (The Peak), and the remains of the thirteenth-century St Saviour's Chapel. The main industry now is the exporting of china clay using modern facilities up-river.

Fowey Harbour from Polruan, c. 1906. You can see St Finbarrus' with Place House, and the harbour front all the way up to Bodinnick. A favourite walk is to go through the town to Bodinnick ferry, cross the river and walk all the way around Hall Walk and Pont Pill back to Polruan and the foot-ferry back to Fowey. It's a distance of about 4 miles.

Ready Money Cove, Fowey, 1954. Just beside St Catherine's Castle, this little swimming cove is accessible on foot to holidaymakers staying in Fowey. Point Neptune House is further along the esplanade to the right.

Fowey Harbour from Mount Pleasant, c. 1910. We look down past the Fowey Hotel, and glimpse the ferry jetty, the china clay ship, and lovely Hall Walk in the distance. There is now a monument to Quiller-Couch high on Penleath Point, behind the schooner. In the top right-hand corner is the wooded creek of Pont Pill, which means creek (pill) with a bridge (pont).

Lovely Pont valley at full tide, c. 1910, with the little footbridge in the foreground. When the old lime kiln on the left was in use, ships would arrive regularly with limestone for the kiln and other items for the local community, and take local produce. You can still sit by the bridge and see kingfishers flit by, with just a flash of blue. If you are lucky you may even spot swans, herons, cormorants, redshanks, wagtails, sandpipers, dunlin or curlew! Most of this land around the creek is now owned by the National Trust.

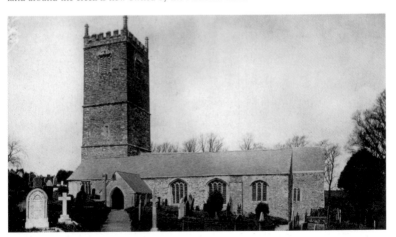

The Church of St Wyllow in Lanteglos, c. 1910. It is a stiff climb from Pont Pill to this isolated church, and it can be a difficult place to find by car! Some of the Mohun family of Hall Manor, who initially created the Hall Walk, are buried here.

Bodinnick Ferry, Fowey, c. 1905. After going through Fowey you can see Bodinnick village across the river. The house on the right, Ferryside, was owned by Gerald du Maurier in 1926, and it was here that his daughter, Daphne, wrote her first novel *The Loving Spirit*. It was also from here that Daphne sailed up Pont Pill to be married in Lanteglos Church. Bodinnick was an important ferry for horse traffic years ago.

Lerryn Creek from the fine sixteenth-century bridge, c. 1910. This is another unspoilt creek further up the Fowey river, and now the National Trust own a large part of the north bank. There is a lovely 6-mile walk from the bridge and along the north bank (right side) of the creek to beautiful St Winnow's Church on the Fowey river, returning via National Trust land.

Above: Charlestown Harbour in St Austell Bay, c. 1900. Observe the outer pier on the right, the tidal basin in the middle, and dry dock on the left.

Charlestown Harbour.

Charlestown Basin and Dry Dock, 1914. Charlestown was originally a small pilchard-fishing hamlet named West Polmeor. Then Charles Rashleigh of Menabilly employed John Smeaton to design and build the new harbour between 1790 and 1798. The objective was to export china clay, tin, copper and stone from local mines and quarries, and to handle trade in pilchards, coal, timber, lime and other general cargo. First the outer pier and a few houses were built, then the basin inside the pier was excavated, and the dock was dug and gates fitted. It was a remarkable achievement because the workers dug out of solid rock using primitive tools, and removed all the waste on mules. The harbour became a thriving port and many people gained employment. Then at the end of the nineteenth century, with a decline in mining and fishing, the work dwindled. China clay was the only buoyant industry and Par and Fowey gained the bulk of this work. Today Charlestown is mainly a tourist attraction. It is a wonderful little harbour and a living memorial to the builders.

Opposite below: Ships loading at Charlestown, c. 1900. The china clay was transported from the quarry to the dockside by horse and cart. Then, with the sailing ship alongside, the clay was tipped from the cart into the chute seen on the left, and into the hold of the ship.

Pentewan Harbour in Mevagissey Bay, c. 1900. About thirty years after Charlestown was completed, Sir Christopher Hawkins decided to build a small harbour at Pentewan to compete for the same trade, and the work was undertaken from 1820 to 1826. The harbour consisted of an entrance channel with a long pier, leading to double lock gates 26 ft wide which gave entry to a 1¼-acre basin with a 1,132-ft wharf, all built to the east of the White River beside the wide stretch of Pentewan Sands. In 1829 a railway was built from St Austell to Pentewan Harbour and wagons were originally horse drawn, but steam engines gradually replaced the horses. In this photograph the nearest ship is on the north side of the harbour basin with railway wagons alongside for a mixed cargo. On the left can be seen the clay-loading berths (or tips) on the south side, with their tramway on a viaduct. A section of the viaduct was pivoted and balanced so that a loaded wagon would tip over far enough to deposit its cargo down a chute to the hold of a ship. The harbour remained in business for over 100 years but then began to decline, and closed after the Second World War. Today you can walk around the pleasant little village and harbour, see the remains of the rail track, the lock gates festooned in bulrushes, and the sandbank that was once the harbour mouth.

Above and below: Pentewan Beach and Harbour, c. 1920. The beach is seen in the top photograph with Penare and Chapel Points in the distance. That is the south side of the basin with the viaduct and the White River beyond. The lock gates are seen over on the left. The bottom photograph looks up the beautiful Pentewan valley from above the coastguard house near the lock gates. A locomotive is just visible on the trestle viaduct on the left.

Above and below: Two views of Mevagissey in the early 1900s. It is 2 miles south of Pentewen and set in a valley which forms a natural harbour. The top photograph is dated around 1930 and the bottom one was taken in 1910. It is a picturesque place with an inner pier rebuilt in 1775, and an outer breakwater dating from 1866. You can sail a boat in and out easily and moor it in the outer harbour at all states of the tide. In the eighteenth century Mevagissey had the fourth largest pilchard industry in Cornwall; this port exported 35 million pilchards a year. In recent times the port has kept busy with craft fishing for turbot, plaice, skate, lobsters and many other fish. The old lifeboat station, now an aquarium, is in the top picture, and there is a museum by the harbour, with pubs and eating places on the quay.

Portscatho in Roseland, c. 1910. The country on the eastern side of Carrick Roads is given the name Roseland, which means 'moorland isle', because the area is nearly an island. In 1910 Portscatho was a quiet fishing village. Today it retains its charm, and visitors come to enjoy the area and see those lovely views across to Gull Rock, Nare Point and Dodman Point.

St Mawes, c. 1930. It has a fine position looking south on a promontory between the mouth of Falmouth harbour and the Percuil river. It's the 'capital' of Roseland and a mecca for sailing and seaside activity of all kinds. First came the Tudor castle of Henry VIII in 1542, then the picturesque cottages, houses and hotels.

The entrance to Falmouth Harbour in 1924. This photograph was taken from Pendennis Castle, and shows the harbour entrance, across to St Anthony Head and its lighthouse on the Roseland side.

Falmouth Parish Church and docks, c. 1930. This church was built in 1665. Falmouth only came into prominence in around 1660, but it soon became recognized as one of the best natural harbours in Britain. It is easily entered in almost any state of tide or weather. The docks were built in around 1859 and they have been developed to include the Queen Elizabeth dock, which takes ships of up to 90,000 tons. During the Second World War the docks played a vital part in repairing ships damaged in the Atlantic. Falmouth was also used as a base for the Normandy landings in 1944.

Falmouth Harbour and Pendennis Castle, c. 1930. This view from Flushing shows Pendennis Head and the commanding position of Pendennis Castle, built in 1540. It was defended by Colonel John Arundell of Trerice for Charles I in 1646, until he was forced to surrender by General Fairfax.

Prince of Wales Pier, Falmouth, 1913. A lovely scene with people crowded on the pier and going on river trips, perhaps down to Helford or just across to St Mawes. It's summertime and the Royal Cornwall Yacht Club has a regatta, and soon there will be hundreds of dinghies dotted around the Carrick Roads, all jostling for position.

King Harry ferry and River Fal, c. 1905. This is up-river in the most beautiful wooded reach of the River Fal, near Trelissick Gardens. King Harry ferry is one of the most ancient crossing places in Cornwall. In those days the traveller would use ferries at Cremyll, Bodinnick, Par and King Harry on the way to Penzance from Plymouth.

Sea front, Falmouth, c. 1905. This is a photograph taken from Castle Drive near Pendennis Point, looking south along the sea front. The big hotel on the right is the Falmouth Hotel. Since that time more hotels have been added and some enlarged, so today it is still an elegant sweep of promenade with a good range of hotels.

Above: Helford village, 1949. It is situated in a small wooded creek on the south side of the serene Helford river. The cottages nestle along the side of the creek in a timeless way. Today the scene is unchanged. Non-residents must park in the car park outside the village and walk around the creek. There is natural splendour together with neat old houses and a little wooden bridge to cross the creek.

Gweek, at the head of the Helford river, c. 1950. It was once an important port, and in the nineteenth century thousands of Cornish people emigrated to North America from here. Earlier, tin from mines in the Wendron area was exported from Gweek. By 1950 the river was silted up and only craft with shallow draughts could reach the port. Now small boats are harboured and repaired here. The two granite bridges carry more traffic, and Gweek is best known for its seal sanctuary.

Opposite below: The Shipwright's Arms on the west side of Helford creek, 1937. I don't know what it was like then, but today it is popular, with locals, tourists and yachtsmen mingling in the bar and garden for a drink or an alfresco meal. I have a pint of best bitter and a pasty sitting in the garden on the creekside with the smell of glorious mud wafting up, while the cheeky chaffinches, robins and sparrows hop on to my plate and peer at me with head on one side, as if to say 'What about us birds then?'

St Anthony in Meneage, c. 1930 (the word meneage means 'land of the monks'). This Norman church of mellow grey stone is on Gillan creek, on the south side of the Helford river. Some believe that the church was built by shipwrecked Normans who were caught in a storm and driven ashore near Gillan creek. They had vowed to build a church to St Anthony if they were saved. There may be some truth in this because the tower is built of fine-grained granite of a kind not found in Cornwall, but which was quarried in Normandy. St Anthony is now a yachting centre with boats thronging the foreshore. We brave the narrow little roads, usually in May, to see the glades of bluebells and the birdlife. Robins sit on your (broken) wing mirror as if you are invisible, and look at you strangely. Sometimes I wonder whether some of my dead relatives come back as birds! If you can find a place to park along the creek, you will almost certainly see a lone majestic heron daintily spearing its lunch on the incoming tide. You may see a kingfisher, or a white swan, or some other fish- or crustacean-crunching creature.

Four

St Keverne to
St Michael's Mount

St Keverne village, 1903. The savage manacles reef lies off the east coast of the Lizard, near the tiny fishing village of Porthoustock. St Keverne village is inland from Porthoustock and the tall octagonal spire of St Keverne Church is a valuable marker for mariners around that coast. There were many shipwrecks on the manacles in the nineteenth century as ships rounded the Lizard and headed for Falmouth, and there are over 400 drowned sailors buried in St Keverne churchyard. The SS *Mohegan* was wrecked in 1898 and 106 passengers and crew were drowned. Their grave in the churchyard is marked with a huge granite cross. The buildings around the lych-gate have now been removed.

Coverack harbour, c. 1920. It is a typical Cornish fishing village on the east side of the Lizard, and this view looks across Coverack Bay to North Corner and up the hill. The village is perched on Dolor Point, with the harbour in Coverack Bay. The Paris Hotel was named after the great liner SS *Paris* which ran aground in Coverack Bay in 1899. A new sea-wall was built alongside the road recently because of storm damage, but the place hasn't changed much, except that there has been some building on the hillside in the distance.

Cadgwith Cove, 1929. This is the most picturesque of the Lizard fishing villages. Here we see the cove with the Todden, a small headland, separating the two little beaches. The narrow lane wriggles its way up to Ruan Minor at the top of the hill. There were few cars to worry about then.

Cadgwith fishing village, 1920. Fishing boats drawn up on the shore and an interesting jumble of thatched cottages, fish cellars, a chapel and the pub: the Cadgwith Hotel. Now there is a car park before you get to the village, and you can saunter around and see the fishing or gig-boat racing, or end up in the pub with a pint and a crab sandwich. On Friday nights there is a sing-song and the locals and holiday-makers sing harmoniously. Mind you, they don't often start and finish together, but it seems to get better as the evening draws on!

Lizard light and lifeboat station, c. 1920. The most southerly point in Cornwall. The lifeboat station has been closed and the Lizard-Cadgwith lifeboat was moved to Kilcobben cove on the east side of the Lizard. There is an impressive tidal race at the Point and a number of named rocks, for example Bumble rock, Enoch rock and Vasiler.

Kynance Cove, 1950. This is on the west side of the Lizard peninsula and is a stunningly beautiful place owned, since 1950, by the National Trust. The cove is a sun-trap sheltered by 200-ft cliffs and facing south. When the tide is out it reveals a vast expanse of firm golden sands. Giant mounds of multi-coloured rock rise through the sand and have names like Albert Rock (after Prince Albert) and Sugar Loaf Rock.

Mullion Cove, c. 1910. Mullion Cove is further around the west side of the Lizard. The west pier was built in 1893 and the south one in 1895. The Lord Robartes of that time met the cost to assist the fishermen. The National Trust now own the cove. Marconi was transmitting across the Atlantic from Poldhu Point, on the cliffs in the distance, in the early 1900s.

Poldhu Cove, 1950–a mediocre-looking cove at that time. The National Trust now own the cove and they have restored it to produce an attractive sandy beach. In the background is the Poldhu Hotel which is now a residential home. Further along towards Polurrian Cove you reach the Marconi monument, erected in 1937.

Church Cove, Gunwallow, c. 1910. This is a very scenic spot, the little church with its detached tower is huddled down behind a rocky cliff at Church Cove. The sand here is largely composed of powdered shells. Just behind the church is Dollar Cove where Spanish and Portuguese treasure ships are reputed to have been wrecked years ago. Now, Mullion golf course is on the glorious cliffs in the background. Golfer John Betjeman coined a term 'to be mullioned', which is when you are taking an important shot at Mullion, get distracted by the loveliness of it all and strike your ball into the sea!

Porthleven Harbour, c. 1900. In the eighteenth century this was a small cove with about four hundred inhabitants fishing, mining, farming and smuggling. Then a harbour was built, between 1811 and 1825. The harbour trade included copper from Godolphin, lead from Wheal Penrose, china clay, tin, slate, limestone, coal, timber and general cargoes. The local mines closed and Harvey's of Hayle bought the harbour and ran it until they sold it to the Hagenbach Trust in 1961. Since 1977 it has been owned by Speyhawk Ltd of Windsor. In the photograph Breageside is on the left (in the parish of Breage) and Sithneyside is on the right (in the parish of Sithney). At the head of the harbour are the Richard Kitto and Jackie Bowden & Son Shipbuilding Yards (left and right respectively). Jackie Bowden was my great-grandfather. On the horizon can be seen Tregonning Hill where William Clotworthy found china clay, and the tower of Breage Church. The shipbuilders have gone but the harbour is much the same. Many of the surrounding fields have been built on, however, so now we have an interesting old centre with new growth around the edges.

Porthleven Bay View Terrace showing Clock Tower.

Bayview Terrace and the Bickford-Smith Institute, 1905. Before the institute there was an old smugglers' pub, the Fishmonger's Arms, on this site, when the place was just a sandy cove. It conjures up thoughts of rough types with patches over their eyes bringing brandy ashore at dead of night. Bayview Terrace speaks for itself really. Up above is Peverell Terrace with the old coastguard building on the left.

Porthleven Harbour entrance, c. 1895. The fishing fleet is grouped to take to sea. The 465-ft pier looks benign, but be warned, it's a deadly place! The sea strikes like a serpent when least expected, and lives have been lost there.

Above: Breageside, Porthleven, c. 1895. Another pub, the Ship Inn (or tavern) this time, over on Breageside, with the seagulls swirling around in their hundreds. Someone has a catch, or are they just serving seafood lasagne in the pub? Mind you, to be dive-bombed by a seagull is no small matter. On the left is the old lifeboat station. In 1895 it would have housed the Charles Henry Wright, a 34-ft lifeboat, ten-oared, with thirteen in the crew.

St Peterstide procession, c. 1908. The ladies all dressed up and parading up Peverell Terrace. Look at all those hats and finery. The festival of St Peter, the patron saint of fishing, falls on 29 June each year. It was a Wesleyan celebration (the Bible Christians had theirs on 30 June). There would be bands in the lead and some 400 people would parade around the village in their best clothes, under silk banners. They would end up in Kitto's Field and eat huge saffron buns and drink hot tea. After tea there were sports for the children and games for the young people—and a bit of courting went on in the kissing games. Later they would visit the fair and ride on the Brewers' Galloping Horses roundabout with lovely tinkling music, and watch 'Jones' Show' dancers and clowns. At the stroke of midnight the organ would play a hymn, 'It is well with my soul', and they would go home with tears in their eyes.

Opposite below: 'Tracking' in Porthleven, c. 1900. Under certain sea and tide conditions the old sailing luggers needed to be pulled along the dockside and out to the open sea. This was called tracking and here we see a boat being pulled along in front of Bayview Terrace. I believe the men are, left to right: Mr Eddy, Jack James Thomas and Robert Pascoe.

St Peterstide procession on Breageside, c. 1908. The fishermen parade along the quay and the fishing fleet lies silent. No one works on St Peter's day. The roundabout is on the quayside ready for the evening celebrations. The men lead the parade and the ladies follow behind.

St Peterstide and dancing, Kitto Field, c. 1908. This is the field behind Fore Street which is now a car park. In 1976 the Wesleyans, Bible Christians, and the C of E joined together for one celebration for the first time. Now the event is held on the nearest Saturday to 29 June.

Going out to sea, c. 1920. This is the fishing boat *Bessie* (387 PZ) leaving Porthleven Harbour with William Henry Kitchen (Snr) at the stern.

Landing a catch at Porthleven, 1908. Captain Will Cowls (with pipe) is on the right. The crew have a good catch.

Five local men on the quay at Porthleven, c. 1920. Peter Kitchen is on the left, with Mr Curnow next to him, and Willie Bawden on the extreme right.

Launch of the *Lady Hilda* in 1909. The Earl de la Warr ordered this yacht from Jackie Bowden's shipyard and named it *Lady Hilda* after his second wife. The shipyard was having difficulty in obtaining further orders, but struggled on until closure in 1912.

Right: John (Jackie) Bowden, c. 1900. Jackie Bowden started a boatbuilding business in Porthleven with his brother, Thomas, in the 1870s. When his brother emigrated to South Australia in 1883 Jackie bought him out, and the firm became J. Bowden & Son.

Below: Thomas Bowden, c. 1880. He emigrated and settled in Port Pirie, South Australia, in 1883. Using his shipwrighting experience he started a successful timber mill and woodworking business there, which is run by his family to this day.

Shipyard apprentices in Kitto's shipyard, c. 1914. This photograph was probably taken during the building of the *Shireness*. Fred Levan Matthews is the fourth seated person from the right. Fred Cowls is standing in the front row second from the left (without a cap). Thomas Pascoe is standing on his left (with cap and hammer). George Gilbert is the fifth standing man from the right.

Porthleven with clock and coast, c. 1910. Looking towards Gunwallow, we see the 4-mile sweep of Porthleven beach with lovely coastal paths to mysterious Loe Bar and the Penrose estate. The building with the prominent clock tower was given to the village by Mr Bickford-Smith of Trevarno estate, to be an institute of learning. In the foreground young and old discuss the weather and the fishing in those sweet singsong voices I remember so well.

Loe Bar Road, Porthleven, 1907. This is on the east side of Porthleven and we are looking west past the beach and pier, towards Praa sands. In the last few years these cliffs have fallen away after some violent storms, and a new concrete sea wall has now been completed. I have included this photograph as a little reminder of 'vanishing Britain'.

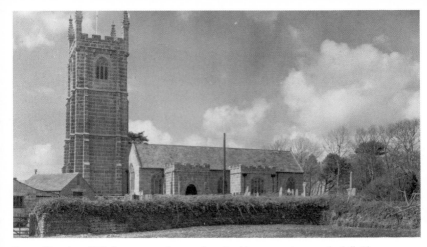

Breage Church, c. 1910. Its tower can be seen from Porthleven, peeping over the hill. The church is dedicated to St Breaca, a sixth-century saint from Ireland. It was rebuilt in 1466 and it is the burial place of members of the famous Godolphin family who lived at their mansion a mile or so away. Sidney, 1st Earl of Godolphin, was Lord High Treasurer to Queen Anne and a friend of John Churchill, 1st Duke of Marlborough. Sidney's wife, Margaret Blagge, died in childbirth in London in 1678 and asked to be buried in her husband's country. Her body was taken by ship to Port Elven (Porthleven) and is buried in the church.

Breage Church murals, c. 1910. Some fifteenth-century murals had been discovered in the church and in 1890 work began to uncover them. On the north wall is 'St Christopher carrying the child Christ' and 'Christ of the trades'. They give some idea of the colourful medieval church interior.

Sithney Church in 1905. The hamlet of Sithney is about a mile from Breage, and the patron saint of Sithney Church is St Sezni (or St Sinnisus) who is believed to have come from Ireland with St Breaca in the sixth century. St Sezni is more widely known in Brittany, where a church at Guisseny exists under his patronage. We go to Sithney for a cream tea at a little place near the church, and sitting there with jam and scones and a big bowl of Cornish cream, I sometimes get a slight guilty feeling!

Praa Sands Bay, c. 1950. A nice sandy bay backed by a few houses. Praa (pronounced pray) has now been developed into a place for family holidays, with caravan sites providing easy access to the sands and long sunny days on the beach.

St Michael's Mount, c. 1920. It has a long history and has been a church, priory, fortress and private house over the years. Legend has it that archangel St Michael was seen on the Mount in 495 by some fishermen. After 1066 William the Conqueror gave Cornish lands to Robert, Count of Mortain, and he in turn granted the Mount to the Abbot of Mont St Michel in France who established a priory here. Henry V appropriated the Mount and granted it to Syon Abbey. Then Henry VIII dissolved the monasteries in 1535 and St Michael's Mount became the property of the crown. It was leased to governors such as Sir Francis Bassett, who defended it against Cromwell's army in the Civil War. In 1659 Colonel St Aubyn purchased the Mount from the heir of Sir Francis Bassett and it became a private house. In 1887 the incumbent, Sir John St Aubyn, was granted a peerage and became the 1st Lord St Levan. In 1954 the 3rd Lord St Levan gifted St Michael's Mount to the National Trust. The 4th Lord St Levan inherited the title in 1978.

Five

St Hilary to St Ives

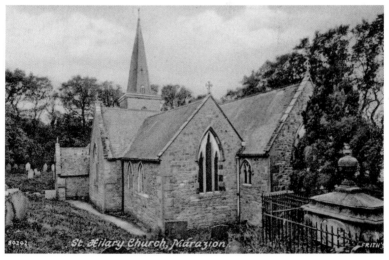

St Hilary Church, c. 1945. The church can be seen from St Michael's Mount. When it was built in the fourteenth century it was under the patronage of the French monks at the Mount, and they dedicated the church to St Hilary, a fourth-century bishop of Poitiers. In 1912 Father Walke was appointed vicar. He was married to Anne Walke, a talented artist of the Newlyn School of Artists, and they beautified the inside of the church, making it one of the most notable shrines in the county. Walke started The Jolly Tinners home for destitute children from London; he was also the author of the nativity play *Bethlehem*. This was broadcast by the BBC, and Walke's appeal for funds for his home was very successful. His teachings were controversial, and in August 1932 a crowd of people gained entry to the church and destroyed the interior with axes and hammers. Eventually Father Walke was compelled to retire. Today the church has been restored to its past beauty.

Penzance & Harbour

Penzance Harbour, c. 1910. We look down over the town and the harbour from the north-east, and the tall tower of St Mary's Church, built in the 1930s, is the most prominent feature to be seen. The church is at the end of Chapel Street, near the harbour which is tidal and enclosed by long piers which jut out into the bay. The South Pier with the lighthouse forms one side of a floating basin. The town was sacked by the Spaniards in 1595 so the buildings date from that time. Then the nineteenth-century development was helped by mining, fishing and the coming of the railway.

Penzance from Newlyn, c. 1920. Looking from the other direction St Mary's still catches the eye and we see the road leading to the Promenade. I imagine that in 1920 the elegant Victorian terraces and the principal streets like Market Jew Street, Chapel Street and the Promenade were little different from today.

Above and below: Penzance Promenade. These two photographs of the promenade show opposite views at different dates. The top photograph taken in 1930 shows a very popular view. The curve of the railings and wide promenade with the church in the background is interesting and attractive. The bottom photograph looks towards Newlyn and was taken in 1906. It has a certain Edwardian splendour with the elegant buildings, the ladies sitting down or strolling along the prom, with long dresses and pretty hats everywhere.

Promenade, Penzance.

Newlyn Harbour Cornwall.

Newlyn Harbour, 1908. A lovely view of the harbour entrance with men on the North Pier as the fishing fleet return to harbour. The local vicar, the Revd W.S. Laach-Szyrma started an appeal to build a new harbour, and it was completed in 1894. It is the largest harbour in the south-west and has a large export trade in aggregate from Penlee Quarry. Newlyn is also known for its School of Artists which was created here in 1900. Today it is the premier fishing port and the main fish market in Cornwall.

Opposite above: Mousehole, 1901. One of the unspoilt little Cornish fishing villages with its narrow streets and granite cottages clustering around the enclosed harbour. Offshore, St Clement's Isle gives some shelter from the heavy seas.

*Below:*The Keigwin Arms at Mousehole, c. 1900. This house was standing here in 1595 when the Spaniards came to sack Mousehole, Newlyn and Penzance. Jenkin Keigwin lived in the house and was killed by a Spanish cannon ball. The Spaniards burnt down every house except the Keigwin Arms, and this Elizabethan mansion house still stands today.

Lamorna Cove

Lamorna Cove, 1900. You can approach it by road, down beautiful Lamorna valley and past Lamorna Inn. The inn used to be called the Wink (they say) because you winked at the landlord to obtain some smuggled gin or brandy! Lamorna Cove is a unique place, with its little harbour and old granite quarry, and there are many other interesting little coves nearby. In 1900 the quarry was working and small ships would arrive to take the granite blocks. Lamorna granite was in great demand and was used in the building of the Embankment in London, a new pier at Mousehole, and the Wolf Rock Lighthouse. Later, because the cove was too small for large ships, they manhandled large blocks of granite by road to Penzance for transport by sea. Today there is no quarrying or smuggling; just a few small boats, and lots of tourists eating cream teas or clambering around the shore.

Porthcurno and Pednvounder beaches, c. 1950. The photograph shows the view looking east with Porthcurno beach in the foreground and Pednvounder beach in the distance. This is some of the most breathtaking coastal scenery in Cornwall. In the distance is the Logan Rock, best-known of the Cornish Logans, or rocking stones. It stands on top of the massive granite headland of Treryn Dinas (Treen Castle), the site of an Iron Age cliff castle. The Cable and Wireless Company laid their first transatlantic cable from Porthcurno in 1879 and subsequently many more cables have been laid. Porthcurno thus became an operating station and training college for the company, with many office buildings and recreational facilities. The telegraph station closed in 1970, but the training college remained until 1993.

The Logan Rock, 1906. The stone weighs over 60 tons and was finely balanced, so it would rock with little effort. In 1824 it was pushed off its perch by Lieutenant Goldsmith (the nephew of Oliver Goldsmith, the poet) and the crew of the revenue cutter Nimble. There was a roar of anger from local people and the Navy Board instructed Goldsmith to replace the stone at his own expense. He achieved this difficult task with the aid of massive wooden shear-legs and blocks and chains borrowed from Devonport dockyard, but the stone has never 'logged' with the same ease as before. If you look at the photograph of Porthcurno beach below, the Logan Rock is the middle peak on the headland in the distance (Treryn Dinas).

On Porthcurno beach, 1910. A closer look at one of the loveliest beaches in Cornwall, with golden sands backed by magnificent cliffs in a bay where the sea varies in colour from deep purple to green and Mediterranean blue. The sand is composed of finely ground sea shells, with an unusual lustre on sunny days. In 1994 the cliffland and beach owned by Cable and Wireless was given to the National Trust.

Minack Theatre, c. 1940. Miss Rowena Cade founded the Minack Amphitheatre on the cliffs near Porthcurno Beach in 1932. The theatre is hewn out of the cliff and some 250 ft above the sea. Productions are staged during the summer months with the magnificent back-cloth of cliff and sea. Evening dress comprises black tie and overcoat at times!

Pednvounder and Porthcurno beaches, c. 1910. This photograph shows the view to the west from near the Logan Rock. Pednvounder beach is in the foreground and Porthcurno Beach in the distance. In the background are the high cliffs with Minack Point in the centre and the headland of Pedn-men-an-mere on the left. The Minack Theatre is on those cliffs now, between Minack Point and Porthcurno beach.

St Levan Church, 1900. The hamlet of St Levan is on a coast road just west of Porthcurno, and the church lies in a little valley where the road ends. This church is dedicated to St Levan, the patron saint of anglers, who is the subject of many legends. He lived on one fresh fish a day which he caught himself, and he would then rest on a rock on the south side of his church. One day he struck the rock a great blow with his staff and split it open. He then prophesied that when a pack-horse can ride through the fissure in the stone the world will end. That's a little worrying because I can walk through it now! The split rock is on the right, in front of the church.

Land's End and Longships Lighthouse, 1920. We pass Gwennap Head to reach Land's End, the most westerly point in Britain. The Longships Lighthouse rises less than 2 miles offshore, and some 8 miles to the south is the Wolf Rock Lighthouse. The Isles of Scilly are 28 miles distant and in between lies the fabled land of Lyonesse which sank beneath the sea, destroyed by a freak tidal wave. Some people are disappointed with Land's End, having expected to see a grand promontory, but I think it is an emotional place, and the sight of ships coming and going makes me think of many fond welcomes and sad goodbyes.

Land's End and Longships Lighthouse, c. 1920. Looking towards America as the fishing boats go by.

Sennen Cove and Whitesand in 1920. There is the sweep of Whitesand Bay with its magnificent beach, and at the west end of the bay is Sennen village. It is scattered, some houses down in the cove and others on the slope above the cliff. A lifeboat station was established in Sennen in 1853 and the small breakwater was built later to allow the lifeboat to put to sea in bad weather. The fishermen fished for mullet and pilchards. Today they mainly shoot pots for lobster and crabs around the many rocks. With the influx of holiday-makers, the locals provide accommodation and there is a scattering of shops and restaurants.

Above and below: Two views of Cape Cornwall at the turn of the century. (The top photograph is from the south.) This is the only headland called a 'cape' in England and Wales. We see old mining country, with ruined engine-houses between the sea and the villages of St Just and Pendeen. On the top of the cape is an old mine chimney-stack which recent owners, the Heinz Company, refurbished before giving the property to the National Trust for safe keeping. Offshore can be seen the dreaded Brisons Rocks, scene of many shipwrecks.

Pendeen Lighthouse and cliffs of Pendeen Watch, c. 1910. The lighthouse and fog-signal station were erected in 1900 to warn mariners around these treacherous coasts, where there have been hundreds of shipwrecks in the past. The area around Pendeen and St Just is honeycombed with old mine workings where men toiled for a pittance and died young.

Gurnard's Head has been like this for a thousand years—a great ugly gurnard fish-shaped headland jutting out into the Atlantic. If you park your car near the Gurnard's Head pub and walk for a mile towards the sea, you come upon it. It is also the site of an Iron Age stronghold known as Treryn Dinas (Treen Castle). In good weather you can see Zennor Head to the east and Pendeen Watch to the west. Gurnard's Head is just one of the places to visit on that mystical road from St Ives to Sennen, otherwise known as the B3306.

Zennor Church and village, behind Zennor Head, 1920. The church was built in the twelfth century and is dedicated to St Senara, a sixth-century Celtic saint. In the side-chapel is the famous Mermaid Chair, formed from two bench ends during a church restoration of 1890. The legend tells how a beautiful woman in a long dress used to sit at the back of the church listening to the singing of a chorister, Matthew Trewhella. One evening she succeeded in luring him down the stream and into the sea at Pendour cove, now known as Mermaid's Cove. On the side of the chair is carved the figure of a mermaid, holding a looking-glass in her right hand and a comb in her left. The carving was done five to six hundred years ago. Beside the church stands the old Tinner's Arms Inn, and further into the village is a wayside museum. The impressive Zennor Head is reached by walking about a mile along a coastal path behind the church. It is another very rewarding experience for 'short-distance' walkers.

neral View,
St Ives.

St Ives, 1920. Positioned on the western end of St Ives Bay, it was already a popular holiday resort and a mecca for artists. It takes its name from St Ia, a fifth-century Irish missionary who sailed to St Ives on a leaf, and built an oratory on the site of the present St Ia's Church, which was built in 1426. The church tower is 80 ft high and built of massive granite stones brought by sea from Zennor cliffs. Inside, the church has a wagon roof and the supporting sandstone pillars have started to lean outwards under the strain. The bench ends are fifteenth century and typical of deep cut Cornish carving. Barbara Hepworth's lovely and rounded 'Madonna and Child' is in the side-chapel. In the background is St Nicholas' Chapel, and to the right is Smeaton's Pier, built in 1770 and extended in 1890. In the centre of the picture is the West Pier, built in 1894.

Porthminster beach and island, c. 1920. The name means 'church cove' and was so called because there used to be a small chapel here beside the stream. St Ives is blessed with three lovely beaches of golden sands, each with a different character. Porthminster and smaller Porthgwidden are safe family beaches, whereas Porthmeor attracts the more adventurous surfer.

Porthminster beach, c. 1910. Fine weather and crowds of people enjoying the regatta day events!

The fishing fleet at St Ives, c. 1910. Note the absence of a promenade and the way housewives dried their washing on the sands. Smeaton's Pier is in the background.

St Ives Harbour and sands in 1949, as I remember it. We sometimes stayed on the harbour beach watching the workers. Mum and dad would struggle with the deckchairs, take off their shoes and socks and sit in the sun. Auntie Flo got the ice-creams, while I buried Uncle Fred —who was never to be seen again!

Barnoon Hill, St Ives, 1909. The photographer looks down over Barnoon Hill and the young people turn to gaze curiously at him. The result is this charming study of Edwardian times: note the slight wariness of the errand boy, the stone, the steps and the lovely background of church and sea. The name Barnoon is a corruption of 'Bar-an-woon' which means the top of the Down. The Down is now full of terraces of houses, and at the bottom of the hill, on the right, is the Barbara Hepworth museum. In the past, the struggling fishing community lived 'downlong' around the harbour (for example on Teetotal Street), and the better-off professional people lived 'uplong' (on top of Barnoon Hill).

Porthmeor beach and island, c. 1910. The name Porthmeor means 'big cove' in Cornish. The Atlantic rollers pile in, one after the other, and surfers on marabou boards play all day. Now the St Ives Tate Gallery is sited on the promenade here, and you can mix culture with energetic outdoor pursuits.

Carbis Bay in 1950 with its excellent golden sands, sheltered from the south and west winds. It is the next beach around the bay from Porthminster. Here the cliff is named Carrack Gladden, which means 'the rocks on the brink'. Lelant is nearby with its part Norman church dedicated to St Uny, brother of St Ia; and along the foreshore among the sand dunes is the testing West Cornwall Golf Course.

Six

Hayle to Morwenstow

Hayle from Phillack, 1960. The town of Hayle, along the shore of the Hayle Estuary, was a major industrial centre in the mid-nineteenth century. There were famous foundries that manufactured beam engines and other machinery for mines all over the world. There were many flourishing copper mines in the district and Hayle was the chief mining port. The high copper prices, the introduction of steam-driven machinery in the mines, and the coming of the railway with Brunel's Hayle viaduct in the 1850s made this a busy place. The mines closed and the harbour now suffers from silting up. By 1960 it had become a backwater, with memories of its industrial past.

Gwithian cliffs and beach, looking towards Hayle Towans, 1949. Some more of the lovely golden sands which stretch from Godrevy Point and lighthouse (on the eastern end of St Ives Bay) around to the Hayle river.

Portreath Harbour, 1906. This was a little port serving the mines around Camborne. It had one of the first railway lines in the world. In the late nineteenth century 100,000 tons of ore a year was coming down this track and being shipped out to Wales for smelting. The mines then started to close and the harbour trade declined and finally ceased. This photograph was taken during the death throes of the industry.

Trevaunance cove, St Agnes, 1910. A small harbour existed here from the early nineteenth century till about 1930 to ship tin from local mines. A more unfavourable place for a harbour is difficult to imagine! Now it is just a beach, with little evidence of its former existence as a port.

Perranporth, c. 1910. It looks over a beautiful bay with firm sand and rolling surf. In the nineteenth century it was a mining community with mines producing tin, copper and iron. Now they are all silent and the remains of old engine houses can be seen on the hillsides. At Droskyn Point the cliff is broken into caves and arches formed by ancient mine workings which have since been softened by the sea. In 1910 Perranporth was on the Chacewater–Newquay branch railway line.

Perranporth cliffs, 1910. There are high cliffs to the south of Perranporth, and a large area of sand dunes inland from the beach. St Piran was an Irish bishop in the sixth century, and the Irish threw him off a cliff with a millstone around his neck. The millstone floated and carried him to Perranzabuloe (St Piran in the sands). Here he built a little oratory (church) and preached successfully to the local population. He was about 7 ft tall and enjoyed feasting, drinking ale or wine, and generally having a good time. He used a black stone for a fireplace and as the flames grew a stream of white metal (tin) trickled from the stone. Thus he learned the art of smelting and became the patron saint of tinners; his feast day is on 5 March. He died at the age of 206 and it is believed that he's buried under the altar in his oratory under the sands!

Opposite above: The Island with its suspension bridge, 1920. It is still instantly recognized as Newquay throughout the world. It used to be called Jago's Island and chickens were kept there before the bridge was built in 1900. It seems to have been a sort of Alcatraz for birds.

Below: The Huer's Hut overlooking Newquay Harbour, c. 1920. Such huts were used to watch for shoals of pilchards, and to alert the fishermen. The 'huer' shouted 'heva, heva, heva' through some form of trumpet (indicating the shoals were coming) and the seine boats quickly put to sea. The huer would then shout directions for the casting of the seine-nets. Newquay had a record catch in 1863 when £20,000-worth of pilchards were netted in one week.

The Huers House, Newquay

Above and below: Two views of Newquay Harbour, c. 1910. Newquay probably takes its name from the new quay built here in 1439. In the nineteenth century Joseph Thomas Treffry (rhymes with reply) decided that he needed a port on the north coast. He purchased the harbour land and erected the north pier in 1841. He was then able to export china clay, lead, tin and copper from his mines, making this an important small port. In 1849 Treffry opened a railway from Newquay Harbour to link with his other mining interests. The middle jetty parallel with the south pier was added in 1872. The harbour was at its busiest in the 1870s, but when steam ships came early in the twentieth century the harbour was too small for them and the mineral trade decreased very quickly. By 1930 the mineral and fishing trade had almost disappeared. The wooden bridge taking railway lines on to the central jetty was demolished in 1950.

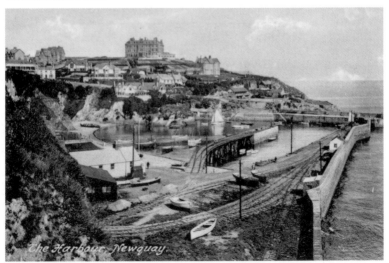

This is Towan beach, Newquay, summer 1930. Opposite the harbour there are the Towan,
Great Western, Tolcarne and Lusty Glaze beaches, and crowds enjoying the golden sands.
The south pier is in the background with the Atlantic Hotel on the skyline. Around
Newquay the Atlantic rollers crash along the shore and provide good surfing conditions. You
can choose from Mawgan Porth, Watergate Bay, Porth, Fistral Bay, Crantock, Porth Joke and
Holywell. All without sharks!

Newquay Harbour looking east, 1903. The Great Western, Tolcarne and Lusty Glaze beaches
can be seen opposite the harbour.

Bedruthan Steps, north of Newquay, c. 1930. The Atlantic breakers crash into these huge oddly shaped rocks known as Bedruthan Steps. They are the fabled stepping stones of the giant Bedruthan who used them when crossing the beach. One of the rocks, the smaller pointed one, is said to look like Queen Elizabeth I, and is known as the Queen Bess rock. More seriously, there is also the Samaritan rock where an East Indiaman sailing ship with her cargo of silks was wrecked in 1846. The National Trust now own Bedruthan Steps, with the cliffs around, and they have a little café there. You can walk along the cliffs, or go down a steep path to the sands, or just stand and savour the wonderful scenery.

Treyarnon bay, 1960. An attractive bathing beach south of Trevose Head.

Trevone beach, near Padstow, 1910. This is a village beach with charming little coves, one of a dozen lovely beaches in this area.

Paddle steamer at Padstow, 1900. There is a sandbank known as the Doom Bar in the Camel estuary which prevents the passage of large ships and, although it's less than one square mile in area, there have been nearly 300 wrecks or stranded vessels there over the last 150 years, including three lifeboats! Some superstitious Cornishmen might tell you that this was caused by a mermaid who got shot by a poor-sighted fisherman, but I have my doubts about that. But this massive paddle steamer has eluded the clutches of the Doom Bar and is a beautiful sight as she edges towards the wharf.

Opposite above and below: Two harbour views at Padstow, c. 1910. The word Padstow is from Petroc-Stow, meaning 'holy place of St Petroc', who came here from Ireland in the sixth century. The town was sacked by the Vikings in 981. Then in the seventeenth and eighteenth centuries the harbour was a bustling port with fishing and boat building and exporting of minerals and cured fish. Its imports included tallow, coal, hardware and timber. Like other Cornish ports, the fishing and mining trade had declined by the end of the nineteenth century, although there was a herring boom later. Today the harbour is better protected with new lock gates and they still have the occasional coaster, but there is only a small fishing fleet now. Tourists come to see this attractive town on the west side of the Camel estuary, and to see the Obby Oss celebrations on 1 May.

The Quay Padstow.

Prideaux Place, Padstow

Above: Prideaux Place, Padstow, 1920. This has been the home of the Prideaux family since the Dissolution of the Monasteries. The monks of Bodmin astutely gave this land to the chief steward of the last prior to avoid confiscation. The Prideaux family were the recipients. They built this manor house on the site in 1588, and have been here ever since. Prideaux Place has a lovely deer park and legend has it that if the deer leave, then so will the family.

323 St. Enodoc Church and Daymer Bay

Daymer bay and St Enodoc Church, 1920. This is one of the loveliest sights in Cornwall. Stepper Point can be seen in the distance across the Camel Estuary and Doom Bar. St Enodoc stands there with its crooked spire. Pretty Daymer bay lies down beyond the church, with Trebetherick village over on the right, and Polzeath bay is further around in that direction. Rock village is just up the river, with its ferry across to Padstow. St Enodoc Church dates from Norman times, although the spire is thirteenth century and the greater part of the church is fifteenth century. About 150 years ago the shifting sand dunes almost submerged the church and in 1864 the locals had to dig it out! Golfers will note the absence of the famous St Enodoc Golf Course because James Braid designed and built Perranporth and St Enodoc courses later, in the 1920s. The church now stands encircled by the tenth to the fourteenth holes of the magnificent Church Course. If you walk through the lych-gate into the churchyard and look to the right you will see John Betjeman's grave. It's just a slate gravestone with flowery old-style writing: 'John Betjeman 1906–1984'. His family have a home in Trebetherick and he played golf here. I think of him on the thirteenth green looking out over the view you see here, and being inspired to write 'Seaside Golf': 'A glorious, sailing, bounding drive / That made me glad I was alive.'

Opposite below: The Old Bridge at Wadebridge, 1904. Wadebridge is about 7 miles up the River Camel, and the great feature of the place is its fifteenth-century bridge. It was built by Thomas Lovibond in about 1468, has thirteen arches, and is 320 ft long. It's a narrow bridge with a number of triangular recesses for foot passengers when traffic passes. The stone for the present Eddystone lighthouse was fashioned here in 1878–82, and shipped from the quay. The bridge is still there but you have to be quicker in and out of the recesses these days!

Polzeath, 1945. It lies in its own little cove on the east side of Padstow Bay. The beach of firm golden sand and safe bathing is perfect for children, with rock pools around the sides for shrimping and hunting 'giant' half-inch crabs.

Port Isaac, 1900. A charming place of steep narrow streets with a jumble of cottages running down the hill. In the nineteenth century it was a busy pilchard fishing port with a fleet of boats, but by 1900 the fishing was in decline. Today it is an attractive place for visitors. There is a good car park at the top of the hill between Port Isaac and Port Gaverne, and you can walk leisurely down into the village. The old school on the left is now hotel, and there are a number of good pubs, with beautiful views over the cove. The small number of fishermen now catch lobster, crabs and assorted fish. Some fish cellars have been turned into shops and other accommodation, but the streets are still narrow and the 18-in Squeezibelly Alley is only for slim people!

Above and below: King Arthur's Castle at Tintagel, c. 1920. Tintagel (from dintagell, which means 'the fort of the narrow neck') is said to be the birthplace of the legendary King Arthur. The ruins of the castle, stretching across the isthmus between Tintagel Head and the mainland, are of a thirteenth-century building where lived Richard, Earl of Cornwall, the brother of Henry III. It is an awe-inspiring sight with the headland towering 270 ft above the sea. The castle was built on the site of a Dark Ages (fourth and fifth centuries) stronghold which may have been a centre for Cornish royalty or chieftains of that time. The Saxons invaded in AD 500 and took over 300 years to conquer Cornwall! So the Cornish must have had a strong leader and he could well have been King Arthur.

Tintagel Castle. Aerial View

*Above and below:*Two views of Boscastle Harbour. The top photograph shows the outer harbour in around 1940, and the bottom one looks towards the village in about 1920. The name Boscastle is derived from Bottreaux Castle which William de Bottreaux built when he was granted the manor by William the Conqueror in the eleventh century. The site of the old castle is now a picnic area. The picturesque harbour was once a busy port with trade in china clay, slate and timber. The narrow dog-leg shaped harbour, deep between tremendous cliffs, is protected by an old pier on the south side, which was rebuilt by Sir Richard Grenville in 1584. The outer pier was built 200 years later. The Wellington Hotel is at the bottom of the hill, and at the top the sixteenth-century Napoleon Inn looks down over the village. Perhaps someone was expecting Napoleon to win!

Leaving harbour at Boscastle, 1920. The twisting and tortuous harbour with its narrow entrance is difficult but the weather is good and the little boat is safely away. The beautiful Valency valley leads from the harbour, and St Juliot's Church is about 2½ miles along it. Thomas Hardy came here as a young architect to assist in the restoration of the church. While here he married his first wife Emma, the rector's sister-in-law, and his early novel, *A Pair of Blue Eyes*, reflects his love for the area. Boscastle is now owned by the National Trust.

Crackington Haven, 1920. A deep valley extends from Delabole to Crackington Haven. The cliffs to the north are sheer, and over 400 ft high, while the southern cliffs slope more gently down to the pebbled beach. It's a very dramatic place.

Above: The beach at Widemouth Bay, south of Bude, c. 1920.

Below: The Strand at Bude, c. 1930. The busy Strand follows a curve of the River Neet in the heart of the town and is one of its most photographed locations.

Above and below: Harbour and beach views at Bude, c. 1910. The top photograph shows Nanny Moore's bridge in the foreground with a view across the harbour to the breakwater. The bottom photograph shows Summerleaze bathing beach at the harbour mouth with the entrance to Bude Canal in the distance.

Above: Morwenstow Church at the end of the nineteenth century. The church is dedicated to St Morwena, who came from Wales in the fifth century. It was rebuilt in the fifteenth century and is positioned right out on the wild and massive cliffs of north Cornwall, just inside the county boundary. In 1834 Robert Stephen Hawker from Plymouth was appointed vicar. He went to Oxford, where he had won the Newdigate Prize for Poetry. When his father could no longer support him in his studies, he married his benefactor, Charlotte I'ans, who was twice his age (he was twenty and she was forty). He got his degree, and the marriage was very happy.

Morwenstow Vicarage.

Old Lychgate and Figurehead of H.M.S. Caledonia, Morwenstow.

The Caledonia Memorial in Morwenstow churchyard, c. 1950. Charlotte I'ans died in 1863 aged eighty-one and was buried in Morwenstow Church. Robert Hawker then married Pauline Kuczinski (he was sixty-one and she was twenty) and they were also very happy and had three children. Hawker wore eccentric clothes and loved animals and birds. He recovered the bodies of shipwrecked sailors and buried them in Morwenstow churchyard. There are forty such seamen from the ship *Caledonia* buried there, and this is the ship's figurehead standing sentinel over their grave. Hawker wrote words to an eighteenth-century popular tune, and the result was the 'Song of the Western Men' or 'Trelawny'. We think Hawker was alluding to Bishop Jonathan Trelawny who was sent to the Tower of London by James I in 1686, and was then triumphantly acquitted. So Cornish men and women stand and sing 'Trelawny' with great pride and passion, as a symbol of a continued fight against injustice. But sometimes, while trying to reach the top notes, I say to myself: 'Old Bishop Trelawny died in 1721 and Hawker wrote those stirring words in about 1850! It was the Revd Robert Stephen Hawker, a Plymouth man, who made Trelawny famous to this day!'

Opposite below: Morwenstow vicarage, c. 1900. Hawker built this vicarage with chimneys shaped like the towers of the churches he had been associated with. It is now a private house.

Trewava's Head, west of Porthleven, c. 1910.

Acknowledgements

I welcome this opportunity to thank those who have assisted me in the compilation of this book. I am especially grateful for the advice and the loan of material from the following:

Mr D. Pengelly, Mr D. Nancollas, Mr and Mrs B. Stephens and Mr and Mrs R. Widdicombe.